ObstacleTo An Obstacle

How To Be Bigger Than Your Struggles

By

R.Z Neal

ISBN: 978-1-949720-50-1

This book is dedicated to:

Everyone who has supported me in my journey. It is also dedicated to the people in the world that deal with any type of obstacle in which you don't know how to get through it.

Table of Contents

Introduction

First, I want to thank you for choosing to be a part of my journey by reading this book. I pray that you will become stronger in your faith and in your trust in God after you read this. Having an *"Obstacle To An Obstacle"* mindset means instead of worrying about how to get through the obstacle, the obstacle has to worry about how to defeat you. It is about realizing how strong you are, regardless of what you are up against in life. Being only 23 years old, I have dealt with numerous things that should not be in anyone's life, let alone someone as young as I am. However, this book expresses the importance of keeping a strong support system, the power of positivity, the value of trusting God, and how to embrace and love yourself.

If this book inspires just one person and makes their life better in any way, then its purpose will be fulfilled. I pray that person is you. I encourage you to be a part of my journey and my testimony.

PART I

Who Am I?

This is the part of my life in which I was learning myself. I was figuring out who am I and who do I want to be. A lot of people in life do not know who they are, and that can lead to a life of making questionable decisions. For me, I had a difficult time doing that as well. I pray you are encouraged to embrace yourself and do what makes you happy after you read this section.

Chapter One: Learning Myself

Generally speaking, every kid looks forward to graduating middle school and starting high school. This statement was also true in my case. However, little did I know high school was going to be the beginning of a journey that I never saw coming. My name is Riza Zaire Neal and I attended Lovejoy High School in Jonesboro, GA.

High school is supposed to be a place in which you find out who you are. I was overweight with very low self-esteem. Me seeing other students with certain things that I wanted and certain girls that I was physically attracted to really drove the insecurity deeper within me. One thing I had going for me was that I was funny. I made a lot of people laugh, however, I had low self-esteem. My being funny got so out of hand that I would take it to the limits and sometimes embarrass myself, not do my proper schoolwork etc. I made people laugh thinking it would help me to fit in.

I was afraid to be myself because being myself is what drove me to be insecure. I was jealous of others and it wasn't what I saw in them. The mindset I had hurt me with my academics. My 9th grade year was a disaster. I had a C-minus average. I found myself in ISS (In-School Suspension) a lot and almost ended up failing completely. I never thought how much of an impact my actions had on my mother. She was dealing with her own issues, including the loss of her mother and her youngest brother, who died one day apart from each other.

The best thing out of all this was I always kept good friends. Two of these friends, Karl Addie and Elliott Kelly, have been like brothers to me since 2005. The impact that these two friends have had in my life is simply unmatched. But I still had my own issues. One day it became really bad. After me doing everything I could, just to be accepted by others, I was embarrassed in a bad way by a girl that I had a crush on. It happened on the bus in the morning on the way to school. I told a peer of mine that I had a crush on her and with me having low self-esteem, he proceeded to tell her himself. Of course, I was against him doing that, but you can't stop someone from doing what they want to do. When she found out that I liked her, she came to where I was sitting, and while standing up, she made an announcement to everyone about how much she didn't like me. She pointed out why she didn't like me. Her reasons included you're fat, lame, have nappy hair, and you're ugly. I was crushed. The girl I liked had just told me she didn't like me, while also embarrassing me. Now, I had to deal with the entire school teasing me about it all day. All I could think about was going home. I couldn't do my work, I couldn't eat, I couldn't function. When I got home, I cried then I cried some more. Finally, the feeling of nobody liked me and the thought of what I was putting my mom through forced me to attempt to drown myself with a note saying, "You're Welcome." The only reason that I did not go through with it was because of my fear of dying at the time. I was too embarrassed to talk to anyone about it. This hopeless feeling was something I just decided to keep inside. After that incident, I decided to keep every internal problem inside.

I was dealing with a severe case of depression. I began to see an attitude change in me. I was known through my childhood as the happy, energetic boy. Now, I didn't want to be him anymore. The only thing that remained the same for me, was my love for music. Music was one of the things that kept me sane. During my 9th and 10th grade year, I started writing songs and wanted to become an artist. My depression motivated me to keep writing. So many artists have dealt with depression and have made great careers from it. I figured that would also be my story.

Many times, we mistake the purpose of why God allows us to go through things. With music becoming a huge part of my life, I would walk around all day, whether at school or at home, with my headphones on. It became mandatory for me to have my headphones with me every day. I was even willing to skip school some days and/or pretend to be sick if my headphones were lost or broken. This was all because I was afraid to interact with people throughout the day. Although these things were going on internally with me, I managed to still play outside, etc. Going outside was another way of me escaping from my own thoughts in a way.

It really wasn't until my 11th grade year that I started gaining more confidence in myself. By this time, my gift of music, making people laugh, and my basketball ability became better known around the school and my community. My skills and abilities helped me make new friends. Although I was still having problems with being myself, I was comfortable with the position and feedback that I received from people. My grades improved throughout each year of me being in high school. At that point, I wasn't thinking big picture about my education yet, but I was happy for now.

I still had many issues like the fear of rejection, the fear of being myself, depression and not fully applying myself. 11th grade was also the year in which I felt a lot of pressure from my parents to get a job. The pressure was so great until it seemed like it was the main household concern. I would apply to job after job, but I just couldn't find one. All of a sudden, I found myself in a situation where I was afraid to become an adult. Graduation was a year away; my family was not in a position in to put me through school, especially with my mom being close to finishing college. I ultimately felt like I was going to be a failure. My trust in God was not strong. I learned you must trust God even when it feels like you have nowhere to go and nothing to do. At this point, the suicide thoughts returned to me. I was afraid to grow up and become an adult. I did not act on any of them, but the thoughts were there. But like everything else, I kept it in and just kept on moving.

Luckily, I entered my senior year in high school. Senior year is the year that every student looks forward to. Senior year is about memories, fun and most of all, graduating. I had a fear of graduating, so I was determined to make my senior year as memorable as possible. By this time, I had gained a lot of confidence,

I was participating in senior activities except for our senior trip and taking senior pictures. Essentially, I was having fun. I even knew what school I wanted to attend and my major. The Art Institute of Atlanta and my major would be Audio Production. So, after senior year passed it was time for graduation. I had dreaded this day and looked forward to it at the same time. The energy was crazy in the tunnel before we walked out onto the field. After hearing all the speeches, before I knew it, I found myself patiently waiting to hear my name. All of a sudden, after hearing the names of others, my insecurities appeared to return to me. Then I heard my name. I heard multiple voices and shouts of cheer. These shouts were not only from my family, but also from my peers. Suddenly, I was in shock. All the hell I went through in high school, I wasn't even sure I would be here. Now, not only am I here, but I'm being cheered and celebrated. It was at that moment that I realized the big picture and how important this was. Sometimes God will put you through hell for you to have a great triumph. With all of my post-graduate problems that were still in my mind, I managed put all them aside and enjoyed my triumph.

Chapter Two: So Confused

Life after graduation was great - the first week. It was awesome to see family friends and family members sending me gifts and money. I loved the feeling of everybody congratulating me wherever I go. But.... that expired fast. It became imperative for me to get a job now, especially, with me beginning school in just a few months. I was still dealing with the same problem, though, no one would hire me. My father tried to help me out by getting my application moved up with the railroad company. I went through the hiring session and had a really good interview. After a few days I finally received an email stating that I was not chosen. Although I've been rejected plenty of times before, this one really hurt. My thought was at my age I could have a great job with great benefits. Plus, I was going to school to learn more about something I love to do. But sometimes, God's plans differs from your plans. We don't always know God's plan. Maybe this is why we get frustrated when things don't go our way.

August came, and it was time for me to get ready for school. I moved in with my dad so it would be easier for me to get to school and back. At the time I did not have a driver's license. That alone made me feel like I was behind in life already. Had I not graduated, I probably would've just said, "Forget it" and made another suicide attempt. Anyway, I started taking the bus to school from Stockbridge to Sandy Springs. I was excited my first day of class. I was around music and multi-talented people in music, photography, fashion and culinary arts. I have always been fascinated being around different personalities, so this school was almost perfect for me. The only problem I had with it was the price of tuition and the size of the campus. It was literally just one building with five floors that students could access. I felt closed in, but I was okay with it because nothing is perfect, and you must make the best of life's opportunities. So, I put my desire for the college experience aside and focused on my goal.

Meanwhile, things at my dad's house were about to become bad. My dad was on me about getting a job. Until that happened, he would give me funds for transportation and food every day. I messed up one day, though. My father has hardwood floors in his home. One day, while on break from school, I was playing around in the house dancing. My favorite song was playing through the speakers. I did a spin move and hit the wall so hard that I put a hole in it. My heart instantly dropped to my stomach and my stomach dropped all the way to hell. Knowing my dad, I just knew it was over. I sat for a while trying to figure out the best lie I could come up with in order to save my life. After I figured out a good story to tell him, I called him. The first time I called, he didn't answer. However, I knew that he would call back on his lunch break. It was at this point that I recognized that God has a sense of humor. I'm sure he does. He made me sit and wait with that guilt, knowing that I just wanted to get it over with. After a few hours, my dad finally called back. He asked what was going on? I told him that I took a shower and while coming out the bathroom, I slipped on the floor and hit the wall putting a hole through it. He was silent for a few seconds. Safe to say, he was upset. I'm not exactly sure of what was said after that, I just knew that there was trouble coming. I had a few hours to collect myself and clean up as much as I could before he got home. I don't know why children tend to automatically clean up the house when they know that they are in trouble. I find that funny. But anyway, after I finished cleaning, I started packing my clothes and all my stuff because I already knew I was getting kicked out when he got home. The moment came and I heard his car pull into the driveway. I heard his car door slam. When he came in and saw his wall, he was livid. He instantly told me to leave his house while yelling out profane language. My dad already knew that my story was not really what happened to his wall. As I walked up the street, I called my mom and told her what happened, she came and picked me up. At the time, I was not thinking about how I was going to get to school. With my break ending soon, I had to figure out a way to get to school and back. I was able to get my license and I started using my mom's car to get to the train station to take me to school. Luckily for me, my mom worked five minutes away from the station. I would just ride with her to work and drive myself there. Then a miracle happened, I was hired as a deli worker at a grocery store near my home. I was so happy. I told my dad just to see if that would calm our tension down. It was not the greatest job, but I was grateful. I finally felt like things were going my way. For a while, I was finally working and going to school. Unfortunately, another spirit found me - the spirit of discouragement. As the weeks went by, I started feeling the negative effects of my job and started becoming more and more unsatisfied with my school. With regards to school, I felt bored, and ultimately, I grew less interested in the whole concept of what I was learning. Happiness was my priority and I lost the excitement that I once had. Work became stressful. I didn't get along with my managers and I was also realizing that customer service was not me. The only part of work I enjoyed was making sandwiches for customers. Reason for that is, I sometimes felt like an artist at work and people were very happy with what I made. It even got to a point in which my head grew big from it. But internally, I was unhappy. So, I dropped out of school. I continued to ride with my mom to work and would just drive back home, go play basketball or just chill at home. It wasn't until my mom checked the mail one day and saw a booklet from my school with the title saying "Exit Strategy" on it that she realized that I wasn't enrolled there anymore. She was furious with me. She was confused with me as well, because it wasn't a secret that I was musically talented. I had made the dean's list in my very first quarter there. She just accepted the fact that school is not for everyone. After everything calmed down, one day my dad called me to just check on me and I told him everything that was going on. Later, in that conversation, he told me that he was going to see about buying me a car. That was the best news that I had heard in a while. Sure enough, he ended up buying me a 1999 Dodge Stratus. Sadly, that did not last long. One day my mom asked me to bring her lunch to work. On my way back to the house, a car stopped in front of me and my brakes jammed. I had to swerve so severely, it caused me to completely tear off my front axle. My car was totaled. I stood outside for hours before a tow truck was able to take me home. I was so confused as to why all these unfortunate things were happening to me. For weeks, I had to look at my car sit on the side of my house. Every day I became more and more depressed and discouraged. Although I managed to still go to work, at this point, I was extremely unhappy with myself and my life. I was also very unclear about what God was doing in my life. I needed some answers.

PART II

What's My Purpose?

In this part of my life, you will learn about my struggles with learning what I wanted to do in life. It is so important to follow your dreams no matter what happens in your life. When you're young, you never want to get to a place in which you are comfortable and scared to flourish. You will also learn that it is important to see your mistakes and take responsibility for them. You can grow from them and become a better person.

Chapter Three: This or That?

While you are young, you are never supposed to get to a place in which you are comfortable. You are never supposed to sell yourself short. For a long period of time, that's exactly what I did. I became comfortable with working at the grocery store, going to the gym and just playing the game at home. I was afraid of failure and I didn't know what I really wanted to do. My passion of making music went away after I left school. I really didn't want to learn anything new, do different things or take any risks. But after some months went by, I grew tired of working at the grocery store. To be honest, I just wasn't making enough money. Once I had a job, my mom made me pay her rent every month, plus I had my phone bill and my car insurance. My stepdad had a lawn service and I helped him out some weekends. Although it was only $40-60 dollars every two weeks, it was something extra. A lot of times it became stressful. There were times I didn't want to go with him to help. My mom was the reason I went a lot. I never been a fan of hard labor. Especially if it required me to be outside.

Later I found a job at a warehouse. This was honestly one of the best jobs I've ever had. The work was incredibly easy and straightforward, I could play basketball on my breaks and the people were very funny and friendly. I was there for a few months but then I was fired. I became lazy and started not showing up for work. I used to ride with my mom there because her new job was close by. I would tell her lies like we called off or the building shut down for some reason when, really, I just didn't feel like getting up. I always had the mentality that my mom was going to take care of me. Like I said before, that was my mindset of being scared to grow up. Eventually I was terminated. It was a seasonal job, so I used that for my cover up of not working there anymore.

I went weeks without a job until my sister told me that she could help me get job with her at a hotel. I knew I had things to pay and I figured it would be fun to work with my sister being the fact that we are very close. That job was very different from what I was used to. I had to dress up, pay a lot of attention to detail, and be perfect in every way. The free food was nice, but I was unhappy there and the environment was terrible. It was mainly management. I had had enough. One day, on my break, I received a call from a cold storage warehouse that I had applied to previously. They called me in for an interview. As soon, as I heard that news, I walked back in the building took off my name tag and threw it at the feet of my manager. We had gotten into an argument earlier that day so that made my decision of quitting much easier. At the cold storage warehouse, the interview was easy. It was almost like they were desperate for a worker. Everything went good there for me. The only problem was, and you can probably guess this, IT WAS TOO COLD! I quit that job during my training week - I went on break, called one of my friends to come get me and never came back. At this point I didn't know what job would work out for me. The good news was, things with my dad had eased up. He would check on me more and I would tell him what's going on. For a few weeks, I was just staying at home. No money, no job, no car, just me thinking every day. I started praying more asking God to help me find my way to do the right thing. One day, I was with my mom at a store and this lady saw me applying there. She pulled me to the side to give me information about a job working near the airport. At the same time, I was also told to come in for an interview at a sporting goods warehouse. I had a decision to make because I couldn't work at both locations because of the hours. I called my dad and I told him about my two job opportunities, and he made me an offer. His offer was that he would buy me another car to help me with transportation. But the catch was that I had to pay the money back to him. I also had to live with him in order to help me save money because I would no longer be paying rent. Of course, I accepted his offer and because the warehouse was closer to his house, I chose that job. He took me to work the first week of me being there. By that next week, I had another car. It was a beauty too, a 2000 Lexus ES 300. It rode so smooth, heated seats, wood grain interior. I loved that car. It was the only thing I was sure that I wanted in life - that's a problem.

Chapter Four: Look In The Mirror

I had a new car, a new job and another chance to prove to my father that I can be responsible. Working at the warehouse started out as fun. I was around a lot of familiar things. My job started giving us extra hours and things were starting to get stressful. While I was there, I met some interesting people. I felt like this one particular person I met was an angel. She kept me encouraged every day and I was blessed by her faith and strength. Sometimes God will send someone to your life just to help you get through things. But one day she left that job and I never heard from her again. After she left I felt like I had no reason to be there. I was good at my job, but I had nothing to look forward to when I went there. Eventually I started not going. By the time my dad woke up for work every morning I was supposed to already be at work. Every time he looked in my room and saw me in the bed, he would question me about why I wasn't at work. I always gave him some excuse like I wasn't feeling well or they shut down the place for the day. After so many absences, I was terminated. I told my dad that I was laid off. Of course, being smart and observant, he didn't believe that at all.

Now I had no way of paying any of my bills. I knew I had to find a job fast. Luckily, I found another job at the grocery store. The pay wasn't great, but it was a way to pay my bills. Things were getting better. The job was easy, and my co-workers really liked me. I actually enjoyed being there. After a month or so, I became really good at my job. I met one of my closest friends there as well. Meanwhile, I began losing weight and living a slightly healthier lifestyle. I was working out more and not eating as much as I used to. My dad tried to get me to save more money, but I was very bad at managing my money. I was very irresponsible during that time. I'm better now but I still have my moments.

One of the consequences for not saving money is not being able to take care of things that happen to you unexpectedly. For example, my Lexus breaking down.

My car started to overheat a lot and eventually I blew my gasket. My dad did what he had to do to fix it, but I had to wait a while before I could drive it again. Around this time though, I just had to go out because it was New Year's. My dad was sleep and I left the house to go eat somewhere. On my way there, my engine popped. Black smoke instantly started coming out of my hood. I was so afraid. I called my dad and told him where I was. He came and picked me up and we towed my car to the shop. The cost to fix my car would be around $2,700 dollars and I was not even close to having the money. Out of the kindness of his heart, my dad allowed me use his truck to get to and from work. During this time, I was supposed to be saving money in order to fix my car. In my mind though, I had a way to work and I felt like I could do what I had been doing.

My dad's frustration with me grew after he realized that I was making no attempt to improve or better myself. I started dating a female that I used to work with and started spending a lot of nights with her. My father would get upset that I wouldn't be at home especially after everything he was doing for me. One day, we got into a heated argument. His words struck deep in me and my emotions started showing. I walked back to my room and he attempted to grab me. When I swiped his arm down, he pulled a gun on me. What still surprises me to this day is, when he pulled the gun on me, I had no fear in my body. It was almost like I wanted him to shoot it. I know he didn't mean any harm, he just wanted to scare me, but anything could have happened. I believe the reason I wasn't scared is because I was ok with dying because I hated life anyway. I was ready for my life to end. After we continued arguing, my dad's first experience with my depression happened. I told him that I did not want to be here anymore. He asked me did I mean I didn't want to be here in his house anymore or didn't want to be alive anymore? I couldn't answer him. All I could do was cry.

After the incident with my father, I started living with my girlfriend at the time. I really should not have been with her. I was vulnerable and I just wanted that feeling of being loved. I ended up scrapping my Lexus after I decided not to get it fixed. I still had a way to work because my girlfriend and I worked at the same place. We were able to get our schedules matched. Fortunately, things did not work out with her. I know that sounds bad but being with her put me in a place in which I was not communicating with my family. I was just being somebody that was not myself. One day I became tired of it though, and I ended up breaking up with her and moving back to live with my mom. I needed to be back in my community, and I needed to try to find my happiness. When I got back to my mom's house, I blamed my dad for everything that went on between us. I didn't talk to him for months. I blamed my girlfriend for everything that went on with us. But ultimately, I was the one who was irresponsible. I was too afraid to grow up. I had stopped praying. As far as my girlfriend was concerned, I was vulnerable. I chose not to communicate with my family. I decided to let her take advantage of me. I needed to look in the mirror and realize that I was the reason that I allowed myself to go through those things. I had to learn how to take responsibility for my own actions. I had no right to go through life blaming the world for everything. It took me 20 years to realize that. The sad part was, I had been taught that my whole life.

Chapter Five: Settling

Now that I was back home with my mother, I felt it was time for me to get myself back on track. I was fortunate enough to find a job at the airport. I worked for United Airlines as a ramp agent. I still didn't have a car, but I was glad that I had a stable job to help get me back on my feet. After a few weeks of working there, my parents found a way to obtain a vehicle for me. It was 1989 Nissan Sentra. Yes, it was very old. However, I was very grateful just to have a consistent form of transportation. I absolutely loved my job there. The people were great, I loved my shift, and it was easy for me. Not to mention, I had a chance to work along with my sister. Things were great. Although, I never forgot my dreams, I had pushed them to the side. All I knew was the airport and trying to save money from working. Once I became good at my job, it was the only thing I wanted to do. I was too afraid of taking any more chances. I was finally good at something, I decided I was going to stick with it.

Although I knew I had the potential to do great things, I settled. I sold myself short. I had learned if you have a dream or a goal, do not settle for less, yet I settled. I knew God had a plan for me, but I still settled. Just because you may not see it or know what it is, doesn't mean you should not try to find it. I was back to being comfortable. There was still much I had to do. I was 21 years old, I had nothing in my name except a phone bill. I was not saving money, and eventually I stopped going to work. Some days, I just did not feel like going. My old patterns were returning to me.

I was becoming bored and frustrated with my job. All I wanted to do at this point was to play basketball. If my basketball buddies were playing early in the morning or late one night, then I would skip work. Why am I not doing what I am supposed to do? Why am I being so irresponsible? Why am I not caring? This was my life. I needed to take it more seriously. I also stopped going to church regularly. Without even realizing it, that was hurting me internally too.

One day, I became low and bored. My mom had always pushed me to apply myself and make something out of myself. Yet I didn't know how, and I was afraid to try. I thought there was nothing left for me to do in my life. I almost gave in to the urge to just buy a rope one day. I didn't want to live any more. Not because I was sad but because life was just boring to me.

Weeks earlier, I was on my way home from work. I stopped at a gas station and there was a guy there pacing back and forth. He seemed very disturbed. I asked him was he okay and he pulled a gun on me. He started telling me about how his family didn't love him and how no one cared about him. I never knew why he pulled the gun on me. All I can remember was me constantly saying "you don't have to do this". After about 2 minutes of saying that, he put away his gun and ran away. My life was spared, but I regretted it because I was so bored with my life. I had no vision for my life and my purpose was blind to me. I truly felt that was

God's plan for my life - to not fulfill my life. I was convinced that I was meant to settle.

PART III

Fight Of My Life

In this part of my life, you will learn about the biggest obstacle I've ever had to overcome. You will learn the importance of having a support system, a positive mindset, faith and trust in God. Sometimes, God's plan and your plan doesn't match, but trust me, His plan is always for the better.

Chapter Six: Wake Up Alarm

A few months after the gas station incident, I went and played basketball like I usually did. As I recall, it was a great day. My team went on a winning streak. I was scoring in a variety of ways. I even managed not to hurt myself which was normal for me. After my day at the gym, I went home, took a shower and took a nap. I was awakened by loud noises in my house. My young nieces were there, and they love to scream. As I was waking up, I noticed something weird. I had lost feeling in the left side of my face around the cheek area. Because I had read that you can actually cause your face to fall asleep if it is slept on too hard, I began to rub it over and over. I had experienced the same feeling by sleeping on my arm too hard. I figured it would be the same, so I just ignored it.

Over the next few days, I was still experiencing the numbness in my face. I started thinking maybe something was wrong, yet I never took any action towards it. Me having an invincible mindset caused me to automatically assume that I could get past anything. I thought to myself "nothing will ever be wrong with me". God knew about my way of thinking. He also knew about me not seeing my purpose in life. He knew that the path I was heading towards would not be a good one. So, he had a plan for me.

Everybody has that one moment of their life in which they start seeing things differently. For me, that day was April 9th, 2018. The day started out as one of the best days of my recent years. I went on a date with a very beautiful young lady. We went to the movies and then to one of my favorite restaurants. I do not remember finishing my food because we had such a great conversation. Everything went beautifully. Little did I know, this would be one of the most important days of my life. I went home and started getting ready for my shift at work that night. On my way to work, I was listening to music like I usually do. I was enjoying my drive to work. Suddenly, as I approached a traffic light turning red, my brakes wouldn't work. My brakes had been giving me problems before and I knew I needed to service them but I was always too lazy to do it. With me not being able to stop my car, it slid, and I hit the back of a semi-truck. This was my first time that I felt vulnerable physically. To make it even worse, my car was not equipped with any airbags. Airbags were not mandatory in vehicles until 1991. My car was released in 1989. I caught the worst of everything. I felt weak but garnered enough strength to call my mother to tell her what had happened. I had to be pulled out of the car and taken to the hospital. As the paramedics rolled me into the hospital, a cop stood waiting at the door to give me my traffic citation. I was discombobulated. I could not pay attention to anything happening. I was taken to the back for scanning. The X-Ray showed that I had a broken nose, a fractured cheekbone, a sprained wrist along with a mild concussion.

Over the next few days, I started to experience trauma. The doctor ordered me to stay at home for a week and rest so I followed the doctor's orders. When

I returned to work, people were checking on me because they had heard what happened. They could also see the effects from the accident which were still on my face. I was in any pain but it wasn't unbearable.

My job at the airport was loud, so with me having a concussion, it made it difficult. Before I knew it, I started having flashbacks from the accident as the planes were coming in. All of a sudden, I started having headaches. I fell to the ground and was taken back to the break room. I made a phone call and got a ride back home. I felt like I was unable to perform the under those conditions, so I ended my employment that day.

After I recovered from the accident, I felt like was able to work again. I found this job near my house at a retail store. This job was just to help me start getting back on my feet. I felt everything would start going back to normal now, but I encountered yet another obstacle. My cheek was still numb. The numbness never went away, I just started to ignore it after a while. Now, though, there was a bubble that started growing in my mouth. At first, we believed it was just an abscess. Once again, it was something that I thought would just go away.

Weeks later the bubble started to become bigger and bigger. It began to affect the way I breathe and ate. Finally, it grew at an alarming rate. With the help of friends at church, we were able to be seen at a hospital. It was hard for us to do it on our own because we didn't have any health insurance. After a few doctor visits, I was taking a medicine to help treat any diseases that I might have. One day, it came to a point in which the bubble in my mouth brought great concern to my best friend and his mother. They rushed me to the hospital, and made an attempt to have me seen for an emergency surgery. I could not have an emergency surgery because it was a tumor that had grown and caused for me to lose feeling in my face. My body had delivered a challenging diagnosis to me on July 30, the night before my birthday.

The following week, I was scheduled for a biopsy. On the day of my biopsy, I was not concerned at all. I just knew in my heart that everything would be okay.

Plus, I knew that prior to my accident, nobody ever saw anything on the scans at the local clinics. Because of this, I believed that it wasn't that serious. They called me to the back and explained what they were doing. I agreed to it all. They cut a sample of the tumor out of my mouth and I waited to see what type of tumor it was. When I returned to the hospital a few days later to receive the news, I was a little bit nervous. My mom is a prayer warrior, though, so my faith was high. The doctor came in and told me that he had the results from my biopsy. Next thing I know, my mother burst out in tears. All I could hear was her crying and it hurt me. I had been diagnosed with a cancer called Osteosarcoma. I never knew why I didn't cry or even feel worried. But I understood why my mom cried. She had lost her mom, my grandmother, to cancer in 2009. Now, her youngest child had cancer.

Chapter Seven: Snooze Button

So now I have cancer. Now I have a disease that has literally defeated millions of people.

Once I left the doctors office. I was distraught. Days later, they set me up to have chemotherapy and to get everything started in order to make me better. God has a way of boosting your faith and sending you small signs of confirmation. The floor I was on would have motivational and inspirational messages every week. However, there was a time that I was just angry at the world. That didn't last long though. The reason for that is, when I let people know about what I was going through, people just felt sorry for me. I never was the type of guy to want people to feel sorry for me. So, through everything, I chose to not let what I was going through affect my mood. I didn't know if I was going to survive this or not. I decided that I was going to either die with a smile on my face or smile through all the pain. In the back of mind though, I thought my invincibility had run out. It wasn't until I finished my first week of chemo that my mind and confidence of beating this challenge had changed.

When I got the report back from my chemo session, my oncologist told me that my numbers looked as if I never even received chemo. When I heard that news, I had the idea that I can and will beat this. Now that doesn't mean that chemo wasn't hard. Chemo reacts differently depending on the person and their body. What chemo did to my body was cause me to lose hair, cause me to lose weight, cause nausea and cause me to be more fatigue. For some reason I couldn't eat hospital food. I could only eat non-cooked foods such as, cereal and ice cream. I couldn't eat cooked foods until I got home. I had to check in for my chemo session for 5 days every 3 weeks.

I've always been a social media person, so I received a lot of support through social media. I especially started to receive support when people saw how well I was taking everything. It was absolutely unreal. I was receiving phone calls and text messages from people I had not heard from in years. Then the next thing I knew, I was being looked at as strong and an inspiration. Ever since I was a kid, I had always wanted to inspire people. I was funny, so I thought I could do it through comedy. I was musically gifted, so I thought I do it through becoming a recording artist. There was even a point in my life in which I wanted to be a professional wrestler that people would look up to. I just never knew which route to pursue. It came to a point where that feeling went away. But, the idea and the joy of motivating and inspiring others came back. I started making videos of me either speaking motivation to people, dancing or just me being silly in spite of everything I was going through. I had the perfect people around me. My church family was and still is heavily supportive of me. My immediate family is greatly supportive. My core friends were supportive and not to mention everybody on social media. Even all of my doctors and nurses looked at me as a miracle. I was giving people hope and helping people get through their struggles just by being myself.

Once my chemo sessions were over and I got the news that it was time for surgery, I was ecstatic. I could finally be done with this disease. One concern that I had was the saving of my eye. When the tumor started to grow, it grew near my optic nerve. Thank God, the chemo was able to shrink the tumor enough for them to save my eye. I was always big on my appearance so, that was a big deal to me. I received the date for my surgery which was December 19th, 2018. My family and I rejoiced when we heard that news. This would be my second surgery since being diagnosed. I had to have a port placed in my upper right chest near my shoulder. The reason was because it was a hassle trying to start an IV in my veins. My veins would just hide a lot. Later, I found out that actually ran in the family on my dad's side. So now, its time for surgery. I was ready. I was well prepped. I was never really scared because in my mind, I would be under anesthesia. Of course, I knew of the risks from surgery. But my faith in God is strong, so I always look for the positive outcomes in various situations. When they rolled me into the surgery room, all I could see was people running around. All I could hear was medical terminology I did not understand. I was lifted onto the table. The last thing I remembered hearing was "Okay Mr. Neal the anesthesia is going in.

Surgery was in process. During those 15 hours, I had no idea what state my family was in mentally. I had no idea who came to support me. I had no idea how the surgery was going. All I knew was, I was in surgery. When I woke up in recovery, I was extremely sore. They told me that the surgery was a success and the tumor was removed out of my face. My left eye was still in my head and the feeling in my face was back. I was just really sore. During my time in recovery, my doctor came in and checked on me daily. Everything seemed to go as planned until one day my doctor became concerned about the amount of fluid that had built up in my face. Just as a precaution, he decided to take a sample of it to test it for infection. Once again, God was testing my faith.

The results came back positive for infection. Although it was not a huge problem, it was problem, nonetheless. Every morning, doctors were putting a needle in my face and putting pressure on my face. Imagine someone getting paid to come into your room and push down hard on your face every morning. They found a way to release the fluid from my face. I knew it was all for the best and to make me well again. On my first surgery, they also placed a tube in my throat to help with my breathing because the tumor clogged my airways. On my 12th day in recovery, they finally pulled the tube from my throat, covered it up so it can heal and released me from the hospital on December 31st, 2018.

Finally, I was back at home and I was so happy about that. I remember going to the gym and making my first three-pointer and even winning a 1 on 1 game. Of course, I posted a video of me making that shot and it received a lot of feedback. People said they were proud of me and that they loved seeing me back on the court. I felt good that some people saw me as an inspiration. God knew that I love to bring joy to people. He knew that I wanted to inspire the world.

God revealed to me to write a book about my journey. It took some time to get started because I knew I still had a lot of recovery to do. I had to get ready for radiation. Everything was set for me to go through radiation. I went through all of the planning process. My doctor scheduled my radiation a few months after my surgery because he wanted me to recover from surgery the best that I could. During that time, I was living pretty well. I was going out and eating well. I noticed a lump on the side of my head, but I just figured it came from the surgery. It would eventually go away. But then I started experiencing pain. I notified my doctor the next time I saw him, and he took action to have me scanned. I was not aware that cancer could come back, nor that it could come back so soon. So, in my head there was no possible way that I had cancer again. I forgot about everything I went through, and the invincible mindset was back after beating cancer. I was not humble about anything. I was sleeping on the fact that God had been so good to me after I left recovery. I figured that the impact I had on people was just a phase. With that being said, I felt God's way of humbling me was having that tumor return and the doctor telling me that the cancer was back after only 3 months.

Chapter Eight: Okay, I'm Up Now

Once I heard the news that the cancer was back, I had a different reaction from the first time I heard that I had cancer. My mother was calm while I was in completely distraught. The only thought that came in my head was "all of that for nothing." I felt like all of the nausea, infection and fatigue that I went through was all for nothing. I even lost my shoulder blade on my right side that they used for reconstruction. I did all that for nothing. I was not looking at it as God was putting me through process. I looked at it as my life was coming to an end. I told everyone that my cancer came back and once again people felt pity for me. But one message stood out to me. A message from my dad. He has always had a way of making me feel strong or making me feel greater than I thought I was. His message gave me the strength to fight again.

Days after the second diagnosis, I returned to the hospital to see my doctor. He felt really bad for me and put the blame on himself. He felt like he waited too long to schedule my radiation. His theory made sense, but I felt like God was not through with me yet. For me, this was just part of the process towards my purpose. I started looking at absolutely everything in a positive way. Anything that came up in my life, I looked at myself as bigger than it all. My doctor asked me if I wanted to just be kept comfortable or if I wanted to fight again since this cancer came back more aggressive than the first time. This was the easiest question I had ever been asked. I answered with an emphatic "YES!!" He told me that I was a fighter and a very strong young man. The doctor proceeded to make the plans for my chemotherapy. I was not worried about chemo at all because of how my body reacted to it the first time I was exposed to it. My confidence was very high. I was disappointed that the cancer came back but I was encouraged by the fact that I beat it once already. I figured the cancer had an attitude and wanted a rematch with me.

I was determined to look at everything in a positive way. It is how I get through life. Optimism and positivity are the keys to success in life. Here I was again starting chemotherapy. Once again, the support that I was receiving was unreal. Friends from church and some family members, who I had not seen in years, came to check up on me. By the Grace of God, my body reacted the same way it did the first time to the chemotherapy. After four months of chemotherapy, my hair was gone again.

It was August 13th, 2019, and time for another surgery. They talked with me about what they were planning to do with the procedure. The tumor was near my skull and it even reached my optic nerve. Once again, the question came back to life - Will I keep my eye or not? Unfortunately, all signs pointed to me losing it. My doctor finally confirmed it. He told me for them to act the most aggressive towards the tumor, I would have to lose the eye. Therefore, I agreed to losing my eye. I would rather lose an eye than to risk traces of the tumor being left in my body.

Because I am a huge Marvel fan, I figured that I would start to look at myself as one of my favorite Marvel characters, Nick Fury. Those type of thoughts kept my mood in a great place. When it came time for surgery, I had no fear at all. I just wanted to be well again. I trusted God for a smooth surgery and believed they would get rid of this cancer once and for all. After 13 hours, I woke up with one eye and most of the feeling on the left side of my face gone. They acted very aggressively towards the tumor this time. Not only did they take my eye, but they had to remove nerves out of my face. I lost half of my top row of teeth along with a hole in the roof of my mouth. They also removed a portion of my skull on the left side of my head. Tissue from my left thigh was used to reconstruct my skull and everything they took out of my face. Now, I have a very long scar and staples that descend from my waistline to about 2 inches above my knee. This was my second time having to deal with staples in my body. The first time was when they removed my shoulder blade in the first surgery. Once again, I was extremely sore. It was worse than my first surgery. It came to a point where it was very difficult to move my arms. It was hard to walk because of the tissue that was removed from my leg. Recovery went a lot smoother this time. I did not deal with any sickness or infection of any kind. I felt like God was showing me favor.

I had to finish recovery, The doctor assigned a nurse to come to my house 2-3 times out a week I also had to complete some physical therapy. I was so weak after everything I went through. I lost weight and my appetite changed. But I was glad to be back in recovery. I would be lying if I were to say that the fear of it coming back did not haunt me. But in those situations, I learned to trust God.

My doctor was very pleased with the surgery. and after six weeks it was time for my radiation. He planned the radiation sooner this time because he did not want a repeat of the first time. My medical team was very cautious with me this time. Radiation was the biggest obstacle I had faced since I was first diagnosed. Radiation was a different kind of beast. My first half of radiation was smooth. It was literally just me laying on a table and have protons target the cells in my face. I did not feel any kind of pain. The whole process took about 25 minutes. The side effects of the radiation was pain, fatigue, loss of hair in the targeted area, lost of appetite, burning skin, lost of taste buds, tooth decay, any many other rare side effects. I thought I would not have to deal with many of those side effects because I was young and the way my body responded to the chemo.

I did not find out what kind of beast radiation really was until the fourth week of my treatment. I dealt with loss of hair, the pain, the skin burns, the fatigue - all of that was fine. The monster I had to fight now was the loss of my taste buds. Mind over matter thinking is true to an extent but this was much more than that. My body would literally reject solid foods. I wanted to eat but I simply could not. I felt like I was starving myself because I could not consume solid food. At the first diagnosis, I weighed 282 pounds. After losing my taste buds, I weighed 170 pounds. I was destroying my health. The doctors were very concerned with my weight loss. They warned me if I kept losing weight they would have to put a feeding tube inside of me. I woke up from my first surgery with a feeding tube in my stomach. I woke up from my second surgery with a feeding tube in my nose. Those were some stressful days and I did not want to relive them. I had to depend on milk to try to keep my weight up. I would drink milk every day. When I was hungry, it was milk that I craved - yet that was not enough. I had an episode one day after one of my treatments, I became dizzy and fell onto the floor. They had to give me fluids.

Days after that happened, I received a burst of motivation from my mom. She told me that she really hoped that the cancer did not come back because she did not think I was strong enough to do this a third time. When I heard that, I started remembering how strong I was. I started remembering all the advice and motivation I gave other people. I started remembering that I was an inspiration and people now looked up to me. Most importantly, I started remembering how good

God was to me. I started eating small meals. To me, that showed me that I was trying, which was most important. It meant that I had the will.

After I had completed eight weeks of radiation. I found myself walking up the stairs, seeing my family and all the therapists and secretaries that helped me through this process. There was a big smile on everyone's face as they watched me ring the bell three times, which signified I was officially finished with all treatment. The day was November 8, 2019. It was that day that I officially became a two-time cancer survivor.

My Message

I know life can seem hard and things can happen unexpectedly. We almost never can be prepared for it. Some of us may even see it as unfair. However, keeping a positive mindset, being optimistic, praying, trusting in God and keeping a high faith level, can help you conquer it all. Those are the weapons that should be used against any obstacle that confronts you.

Do not let anything move you away from who you are, no matter how extreme the situation may be. Have the mindset that I am bigger than my obstacle. God already has our life planned out. He planned it before the thought of you being born came about. He will not steer your life in the wrong direction. Even when things seem dark and you just want it all to end, remember that your process is still yet to be completed. Trust God and know that everything that you go through is for the better. Keep a positive mind and a righteous heart. For every obstacle you defeat, you become stronger. Get to a point in which you cannot be defeated. Use your weapons and become undefeated.

Acknowledgments

My only acknowledgment is to my Father in Heaven. He kept me from causing hurt to myself. He kept positive people around me by placing them in my life and by helping me remove those I saw as toxic to who I am and to my purpose. His allowing these obstacles in my life helped me open my eyes more. He gave me an amazing family, friends and hidden angels - all placed in my life to help guide me to the right path.